Petrichor

Shrividya Mukherjee

BookLeaf Publishing

India | USA | UK

Presentation by *BookLeaf Publishing*

Web: www.bookleafpub.com

E-mail: info@bookleafpub.com

ISBN: 9789363316782

First edition 2024

To the ones in the middle of an ocean

When the tides go high

When you really need the shore

I hope you pass this by

With gratitude,

Shrividya

ACKNOWLEDGEMENT

My heartfelt gratitude to the divine power and grace that have nourished and nursed me throughout the journey.

I would like to sincerely thank three superwomen in my life, without whom this journey wouldn't have been possible. First, my mother. She has been the greatest pillar throughout this journey of writing poems.

Second, my English teacher, Babli ma'am. I began writing under her guidance eight years ago, and I couldn't have reached this day without her profound impact on my life.

Third, my English teacher, Praveena ma'am. Her presence has always been felt in every newly written poem in this book, as she's much more than a guiding star who lit the road throughout.

I take a moment to thank my maternal grandparents who reside inside of me today. Despite their physical absence, I've felt them between words and between worlds.

My paternal grandparents have also shown me another dimension of life, and I'm deeply grateful to them as well.

I would also like to wholeheartedly thank my math teacher, Saraswathi ma'am, without whom chasing my dreams would be far beyond reach. My sloka gurus, Greeshma aunty and Uthra mami have been instrumental in shaping me, and I am deeply grateful to them.

Heartfelt thanks to my classmate Krithika, who has become a subtle yet significant source of comfort for me. Our insightful perceptions of convoluted poems definitely have an impact on the poems in this book.

I owe a great deal to my senior, Smrithi. I believe that during our very first conversation, her unintentional encouragement sparked the idea of me writing a book, and that inspiration has stayed with me ever since. Despite our brief interactions and limited conversations, I am deeply grateful to her for manifesting this feat on my behalf.

PREFACE

I aimed to write poems inspired by daily experiences, with the belief that everyone can relate to at least one instance in their lives that resonates with my work. While some people appreciate the depth of words and enjoy poetry, others may struggle with its subjective nature. With these contrasting perspectives in mind, I endeavored to approach my writing in a new light.

My usual poems carry a hint of melancholy, but this time, I challenged myself to explore different themes. As I listened to my inner voice, I realized that everyone has stories to share and stories to hear. Amidst my busy days, I took moments to quiet my mind and tune into the whispers of my heart. The bond between myself, my writing, and my emotions deepened over time, birthing my "heart-child," Petrichor—a collection reflecting the myriad shades of overwhelm that we all experience.

To my readers, I urge you to take your time to ponder the emotions woven into each poem. Each piece is a product of the profound thoughts that traverse my mind daily. My aim was to make the book relatable to all, recognizing language as humanity's greatest gift. I believe that poetry, in particular, transcends boundaries, imprinting words directly onto the human heart.

I encourage you to explore my intentions with a touch of your own experience and at your own pace by humming the poems or even reading them aloud.

The book comprises thirty-one diverse poems, each a fragment of a sixteen-year-old's musings. Who knows what joy you might discover or where your musings may lead you when you immerse yourself in my world?

To Be Able to Learn

To be able to learn is to be able to grow
To bring the kid in you alive
To be able to learn is to be able to flow
Like the swarm of bees in the hive.

To be able to learn is to be able to share
All the lessons inside and outside
To be able to learn is to be able to care
For everyone you know can thrive.

To be able to learn is to be able to beautify
Things in hues of black and white
To be able to learn is to be able to satisfy
Who you are through day and night.

To be able to learn is to be able to cheer
Everyone who needs that jerk
To be able to learn is to be able to appear
And author someone's work.

We are here to be able to learn and grow
Learners, as we're called
To learn, take a book, learner's heart, and roar
Coz the world of learners enthrall.

Silence

Sometimes silence is all you got to say
Coz there are no answers
Or because of the humdrum spread outside.
Also because the ears are deafened enough to
not hear.
Sometimes silence is all you got to say
Coz not everyone understands what you speak
Or someone might understand without you
speaking.
Sometimes silence is all you got to say
Coz some are captious and others make fun
While you really got to say something.
Sometimes silence is all you got to say
Coz not everyone is worth listening to you.

Silence is a poet's secret weapon
Locked between the ink and nib
It's all that comes out that really makes a mark
Rest all being simply futile.
While silence is not the rising sun,
That catches your heart every morning,
Silence is what shines at noon
When everything else withers.

Petals Feather

I built a feather out of petals
And it tried to fly
Not once, not twice, but many times.
Every time it flew, it soared to the ground
Why?
Is my love any lesser?
Am I not the right hand?

It's three hundred and sixty-five days later
I found the same petals
But the feather no longer exists
Birds peck on them little by little
And fly away into the empty
What my petal feather couldn't do.
Perhaps it isn't made for flying
And hence, I let it lie on the ground–
The place it belonged to.

Life Clock

In the heart's silent chambers, there ticks a clock
Measuring moments in steady, rhythmic knock.
Life's clock–relentless; its hands forever spin
Counting our days from when we begin.

With each passing second, a heartbeat's drum
Echoing the journey that's yet to come.
From infancy's dawn to youth's hue
The clock marks the chapters, old and new.

At noon, ambition dances in the sun's embrace
Dreams take flight; hopes find their place.
The clock's hands move swiftly, chasing the hours
As we strive for fame amidst life's lovers.

But evening draws near and shadows grow long
The clock's ticking whisper sings a poignant song.
Memories and lessons etched in time's embrace
Moments of joy and tears we trace.

And when the clock's final chime fills the air
Leaving behind echoes of moments rare.
We'll pause and reflect on the life we've lived
The love we've shared, the gifts we received.

For life's clock ticks not in vain or haste
But measures the beauty of each moment
embraced.
So cherish the seconds, the minutes, the years,
For in the rhythm of life's clock, eternity
appears.

The Perfect Timing

The planet is blessed, and you are born,
And sometime later, you shall be gone.
Between what lies are the right's and wrong's,
This is the truth of every life's song.

You meet many; some stay, some leave,
Yet in the end memories, memories weave.
Make sure they're not, no grieve,
Coz the time is less and you should leave.

You might say what happens is unjust
And that the ones full of lust–
Get what you don't, and you lose trust,
But the story, I tell you, is at its crust.

What is yours might not be too,
Coz the divine timing has much to do.
You choose to stand by what is true,
And what is meant will come to you.

Now you might question the divine time,
And say that everything you get is after nine.
And you missed the bus coz you weren't on time,
But a little delay is never a crime!

You are taken care of behind the scenes,
And what you see might be just a screen.
Of all the work that happens between,
You and what you are supposed to be.

Everything happens just perfectly
Today you might not agree with me
But when come you back to see
You were just where you were meant to be.

People and places got perfect timing,
And we're bells, to the perfectness–rhyming.
To whatever's coming, we're merely miming
And surrender to seeing yourself vibing
------- To the perfect timing!!!!

You

Lost in the labyrinth of life's winding way
Seeking a path where dreams hold sway.
Amidst the chaos, where voices vie
Find yourself beneath the moonlit sky.

In the silence of solitude, listen close
To the whispers of your heart's gentle prose.
For within you lies a universe untold
A treasure trove of stories waiting to unfold.

Cast away the masks society demands
Embrace your essence in open hands.
The journey within—a quest sublime
To discover your truth in the sands of time.

Amidst the noise, find your silent core
Where serenity dwells, forevermore.
Let your spirit soar on wings unfurled
As you navigate the depths of your world.

Embrace the quirks, the flaws, the light
For they weave the tapestry of your might.
In every stumble, in each mistake
Find lessons learned and not hearts to break.

Embrace the journey, the highs, the lows
For in every moment, your true self glows.
Find yourself in laughter's joyful sound
In tears shed on sacred ground.

So dance to the rhythm of your own beat
In life's symphony, take your seat.
For in the journey of discovery, untold
You'll find yourself, precious and bold.

Lavender Purple

Lavender purple
Petals yet subtle
Dreamt of the Angel's wand.
Asked the cactus
How he lacks fuss
Amongst the bonds unfond.

The cactus then said
"My petals are dead
In the world–desert.
But the thorns yet remain
Not to give pain
But to save myself from hurt."

Be

A tea to someone's toast
An umbrella in a rising storm
One breath to the dead, almost
A hug at night as warm.

A leaf for the moth's growth
A shoulder to cry upon
Love to the ones who loathe
Sunray for the ones at dawn.

If this life so long
Has something little to do
Be the hand you'd long
If that storm hit you!

An Ode to You

You've been strong till here
When all seems grueling
You stayed honest, my dear!

You've been who you truly are
And you know how much it takes
To stand up when truth seems far.

You might be deprived today
But be assured of what you learnt
That truth chases, never fades away.

So pat your back and thank yourself
That you came this far with your truth
Let nothing else stop oneself.

I'll tell even if others have not
You are a champ coz of who you are
There is victory, and that you got.

The Tale of Chessboard

I say life is a chessboard
Initially, you've your moves that roared

The knights and bishops and rooks
Some of which are crooks.

And lemme tell, you've your pawns
The little ones, nothing to depend upon

You've within yourself your army to fight
But as you continue to fight

You lose your army
You scream, "This is harmy"

You lose your bishops and rooks
In denial, your head you shook

And then comes the queen
As you're lured by its sheen

And beauty and fame
Everything she got to her name.

And as your moves get better and better
You're ignited and that go-getter.

You fall in the queen's lust
As she smashes you like dust

Without your knowledge or approval
And makes you very minimal

Little by little, she moves the board
And wins herself, and high she soars

Yet powerful is a pawn
Who traps your queen like a fawn

Is trapped with its own little horns
In dismay, you are about to scorn

As you lose your queen---
Your pride, your sheen, isn't it?

You and your only pawn on the board
To go step by step to the abode

Of where your opponent lies
To only go wry and wry

Only to realize you're a speck of dust
And that loss is a must

When just a mere pawn stands with you
There isn't much you can do.

Once you'd your army of fifteen
And now you lost even your sheen.

"But the pawn is enough" – you console
Though nothing is in your control.

As she fights enough to keep you on the board
You start losing your initial roar

But she ends up giving her life
You then realize you're engulfed in strife.

You're at the corner of the board
But your breath slowly slowed

The same corner of where you belonged once
With pride, but now to renounce

Then, with the army of fifteen
Now ill and fatigued and lean

Yet the world has not a care
It will never dare to spare

And at last, you're checkmate
And that move is always the fate–

If you choose to fall in lust
You're simply a speck of dust.

Duality

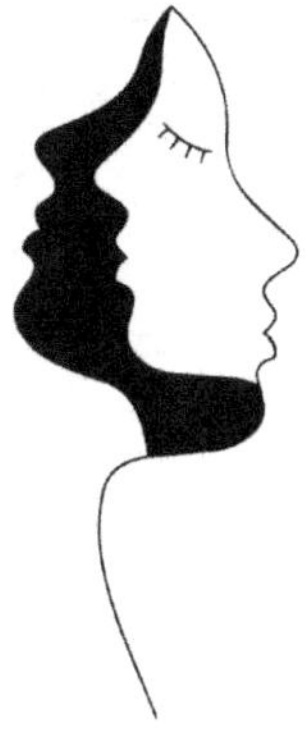

In the heart's chambers, a silent symphony plays
A dance of hues in life's enigmatic maze,
The duality of emotions, a timeless tale unfurled
Where joy meets sorrow and love embraces the
world.

Where day meets night's gentle sigh
Whispers of longing in a starlit sky,
Hope in whispers, fear's shadowy embrace
The duality of emotions, a delicate grace.

In laughter's echoes, tears find their quiet place
Amidst the chaos, serenity's gentle trace,
Courage in vulnerability, strength in surrender's
hold
The duality of emotions, a story untold.

With each heartbeat's rhythm, a melody
profound,
In every tear shed, strength is found.
For in life's dualities, our souls find their flight,
In the highs and lows, life finds its light.

What If?

What if everything around is as you wish
A fragment of your nightly dreams?
And you wake up the next morning
To find the lustrous flowing stream!

The stream that passes by your heart
To show how pure and lit you are
Would you still doubt like today
And push the near very far?

The far that belongs neither to you
Nor to the dreams you finely built
Then why the unwanted doubt and question
That puts you in a wheel of guilt?

Despite the guilt, things are yours
Just the way you want them to be
Then can you wake up the next morning
The mighty dream, can you see?

Your dream might be true or not
But you can still continue to strive
And one day you can see that stream
Passing by to see you smile.

Smile not coz your dream is true
But for you mustered courage to dream
Remember that's what matters as that morning
Might be closer than it seems!!!

Sunset and Moonset

Look at the sun today.
It rose as a shining star this morning
To wake you up
It burns itself to help you grow
The trees grow and the flowers bloom.
It's time for it to set
Perhaps it lived its day
To whatever it could
Now, it's time to depart.

Now look at the moon
It rises as the only source
To ebb the darkness
It fills the night with gleam.
Yet it knows,
How little it's valued while the sun's back.

The next morning, the sun's back
The moon sets simultaneously
Lost existence with nothingness left.
But does it ever lose hope?
Does it ever say 'no' to coming back?
It shines bright at night
(When it's the right time).
And entwines a perpetual understanding
Between the sun and the moon
To shine and to dim
Yet coming back with grace.

The sunset and the moonset
Is a set of two coins on the board
None being any lesser
None being fake
As they shine when they need to.

"It might not be the time to shine
For dim light is suffice, and that's fine."

Resilience

Through trials, fierce resilience gleams
On the darkest nights, it fuels our dreams.
With every blow, it stands tall
A beacon strong, it conquers all.

In hearts that ache, it finds its way
Through storms and fears, it holds the sway.
With courage bold, it lights the path,
Resilience triumphs in the aftermath.

Oh! Boatman

"Oh! Boatman," I cried in pain
"I tell you, my life's in vain
Take me to the other shore
That's the only decision sane."

"Oh! Boatman!" I yelled in fear
"I tell you, there's no peace here
The ghat, there is tranquil enough
The shore on this side is very mere."

"Oh! Boatman," I plead and weep
"There is no seed here to reap
The land there is much fertile
That shore is my only keep."

There cries another young bride
Yet at the opposite side
"Oh! Boatman, take me to the other shore
I got to keep my jewellery hide."

Curtain Falls

All the world's a stage
And I am an actor.
In attires shiny and vibrant
I stood there to welcome my audience
Into today's night show.
As the curtain rose
I heard invigorating claps.
And entries and exits on the stage
I was adorned sometimes
And scorned off at another.
I moved back and forth to deliver my dialogue
Passion in my heart
Sharpness in my throat
And tears in my eyes.
I merely acted as my role
And earned salutes from many.

As it ended
I stood amongst the crew
The claps lessen
The hoots lessen
Coz all know that the play's over.
I bowed down to the people
And touched the stage for–
The very last time.
The only act, and I gave it my best.
Retired as an actor with a smile
All I said is
"You did it, champ! And it's over. Simple."

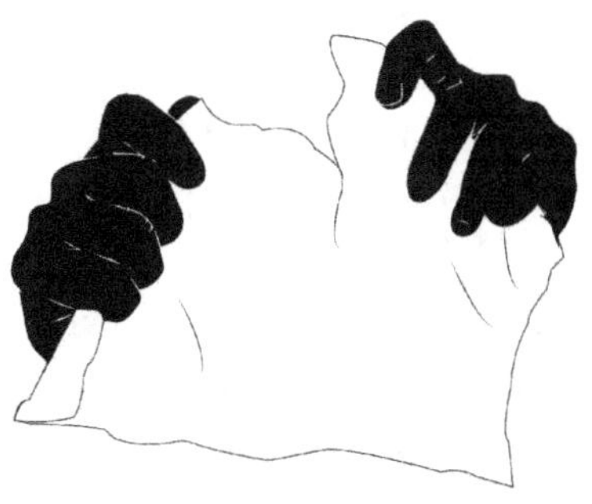

Child

How beautiful is it to be insane
Or innocent or childish?
To run on the fields with no other thought
Create ripples in water!

How meaningful is it to be unmatured
Or naive or juvenile?
To crave that balloon and candy
Love the sound of the raindrops!

How skillful is it to be silly
And irresponsible and creative?
To paint that monotonous landscape
And get a 'star' from the teacher!

How cheerful is it to be relaxed
Knowing everything's taken care of?
Chuckle with all vigor
Despite the day and the hardships!

In the end, dear 'grown ups'
It's good to be lunatic and mad
Just to go with the flow
And find the latent child inside!

Perhaps we aren't as old as we seem
Our hearts ever made of an infant
Just give time to grow
A child's heart in an adult's mind!

A Woman at Fifty

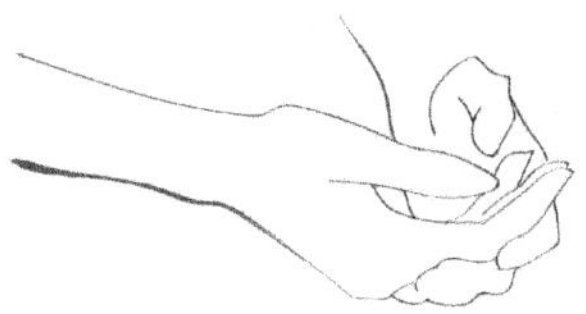

Growing old

It's not that hair grays and we live on pills
We fail to sprint and catch the butterflies
And then we grow old.
Being old isn't today's happening
Of entering fifties.
Old is when I cease to learn
Cease to live and cease to love.
I am a day older
Older by thoughts, deeds, and actions.
A whole day back into the bygone days
By the bygone people.
This was a happening of growing old
Yet I look forward to learn
To foster in me the childlike heart
To spring with the energy I had decades ago.
To ripple water and run the fields

To suck the candy and crave the balloon.
Yes, I am a day older
But I choose to see myself beyond my age
I look at my wrinkles
To feel how special it is to be a child—at fifty.
So, I go through my fifties
While growing through my recollections.

When Dusk is Long

When dawn is far and dusk is long
When there's less right and more wrong
When night feels darker and day's far
When you might not be who you're.

Just know that the wait is worth
Something special is taking birth
Everything you need takes a while
And all you do is wait with a smile.

Sometimes there's little to do
But much to surrender to the spirit in you
The spirit to get back things in place
Meanwhile, spend time in solace.

Though toil and efforts reap results
Sometimes you don't need tumults
A little wait for a gentle embrace
To find your day at your own pace.

Cocoon

Build yourself a cocoon
To armor you from the outside brutalities.
It takes a lot to shield yourself,
Go against the world
And shell from the thunder.
But I tell you, it is worth it.
To be able to live and love from that cocoon
Is an art to be mastered
Confluence of kindness and harshness
Is required for you, little silkworm
You are too gentle for this cruel world
With endless penalties for the victims.
While you choose to fight
With valor and rage

Have with yourself
A tight, cozy cocoon.
And sleep a good night's sleep each day.
Free from insecurities.
Be the silkworm for a while, at least
Till you take flight
As that mighty silkmoth.

Petrichor

I saw the sky with an amazing gaze–
It was sunny and worth a praise.

Suddenly I saw the air smoking
As though a war horse was evoking

All the anger it had got
And soon the sky turned distraught.

Choking in the midday's light
The sky teared up at one sight

And pour and pour and pour the drops
And destroy all the very young crops.

Thunder here and thunder there
And anything alive was a scene so rare

Rains and hails and gales around
Screams and bolts–the only sound.

"Oh my god, a terrible sight."
I said to myself, and I was right.

Everything got gushed outside
Every pain from within cried.

"Why this injustice?" I asked the drops
We are really tiny tots

In comparison to what you're
Violent and fierce, everything's now jarred.

Flooded houses and flooded streets
Flooded and blooded all the feet.

Yet hussshhhhh, the burst of another tank
"Oh my god, why play this prank?"

One over other stumbled on the floor
As each other bangs the doors

The doors that humans chose to close
The environment—is the door everyone vows.

To keep the planet clean and green
And build a bridge between

Nature and humans, they took an oath
As the water now was becoming a froth.

After the oath, someone tries
To bang the door under the dusted sky

And say, "Stop the rain, stop the rain!"
And it tapers gradually, and all exclaim.

"The rain is gone and all is fine
But what we did was a crime

And we should keep up our vow
And never let Mother Earth low."

That's when the petrichor rose
From the earth's heart as a prose

To reflect upon the days and nights
Under bright sunlight or starry skies.

A result of the tumult caused so much
I am in awe of its fragrance such

Though its origin is rugged and harmed
Petrichor has its own charm

And we experience the oneness
Of both joy and sadness

Of the clangor and the serenity
That reverberates for an eternity

How blessed can we souls be
To embark on this human journey?

To Not Care

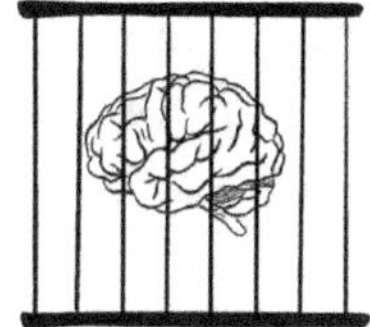

To not care about the ones who don't deserve is
an art
And I think
I am an artist.
It was a long time ago
Perhaps when I was much younger
I thought and dreamt and envisaged a life with
you.
I thought you told the truth and loved me for
who I was.
Not only the truth, but you also told me of our
dreams
And you'd travel with me an inch closer to them.
It took me sunrises and sunsets together to gain
Maturity through pain
And lessons from torn pages.
And all that care I kept for you
Is not my past just because I moved on,

Not my present, as I am older–much older,
Not my future, as my vision is tattered and I
don't know how to fix it.
That care is safe in the safe of my soul, my
reality.
But of you, the one I dreamt of the most, I have
chosen to not care, as there are many more
sunrises I will wake up to.

The Yesterday Song

Yesterday showed you faces
Few embedded in your veins, and few others
piercing your throat.

Yesterday took you to places
And you wished you could hold on to that
serenity like the creeper.

Yesterday marked the entry of the storm
As you saw yourself at the center of the enraged
eye.

However, yesterday made you warm
Even though everything around is harnessing the
little pints left.

Yesterday is far bygone now
And all it gave you is memories or dread, no
longer to live

As today is the day of marking
And all its giving is a part of living, for once

Today is gone into the thesaurus of yesterday
It's either a memory or a shock or a page that
never lived at all.

When The War Is Over

When the war is over, do you still feel the loss of
blood from your wound?
Has the throbbing heart eased a little, or does it
still pounds faster?
Do you still feel voiceless, or do you speak?
With muffled voices?
Can you see the distant land where you used to
live?
Or is it covered by an immovable layer of dust?
After you've met destruction, the end, the death
of many, and you (maybe)
Do you feel like living or just bowing down to
what's gonna befall?
If I ever gave a choice between life and death,
when all you can see is a heap of flesh
Would you choose to live with extinguishing
breaths or die with an abundance of it?

Thirty Numbered Days

It's been a month. Thirty numbered days
Do you still remember me?
Are the memories still with you? Or are they
stolen away?
Does that picture still hang on the wall?
Or is it shattered by the wind?
Shattered by everything that the numbered days
encountered?
Do you still feel my touch and my breath?
Or is it numbed by the dust devils on the road?
Can you hear my laughter and sense my eyes:
the dreams?
Or are you blinded by the thirty-numbered days?
Do you still sing the song we composed? And
dance to its tune
Or is it muted by the noises of the
thirty-numbered days?

Are we still alive to each other,
Smiling, singing, and celebrating?

Are the thirty-numbered days enough to smog
our beauty?
Fill it with crackling winds
Why can I hear the door screeching?

The door that opened to you one day–now
Ghosted and sacrificed and rusted.
Why is it that I feel haunted, as though you are
far away,
Left me in the vastness of the unimaginable,
I lie crumbling to the ground!
Why did you become my past so soon? Is this
what we were destined for?
As I tremble down the memories, you drift away
as the nocturnal flower.

A smash here and a smash there
Can't you hear me still?
I have come to the door you chose to ghost–this
time: mangled
Knock and knock again. Why don't you open
the door?
Why is my nightmare getting truer? Have you
really ghosted–
In the thirty-numbered days?
The truth can't be truer than this.
You need to open the door–for yourself, if not
me.
I'm sure that thirty-numbered days aren't
enough.
You're sure as well.
Do you want me to die thirstier than this? Beg of
you

Open the door.
I want to peruse the magnificent creation one
last time.
You remember me–I remember you
From the thirty-numbered days. I am waiting to
knock for the last time.
Make peace with what I'm left
Then becomes a part of the void.

The Best is to be Better

I am here today, after many attempts to be the best,
after many days of the calendar moving on, languid
of my tiredness, after many tomorrows ruined for
what happened yesterday, after many confessions I made
to the mirror of how I want to be the best,
after many rejections, many voices in and out of
me, do I realize–
realize this arcane truth

I realize it was never meant to be the best
but to be better in whatever I am doing,
better than who I was yesterday
and to be better is the best in life, hence I say.

As per the Prophecy

As per what the wise men said
Who apparently fulfilled this human life
"Do what makes you happy
And smile when you're nearly dead."

But if my only joy in life is you
Even if you're in fragments
I eat and sleep and long for what's past
Do I have much to do?

If my only truth is a big, fat lie
Under the footprints of thousands.
And all I do is an offering to you
Don't I've a right to cry?

If you and I are synonymous
And to do for myself is to do for you

Then tell me, wise man
Doesn't joy in life become anonymous?

Broken Silence

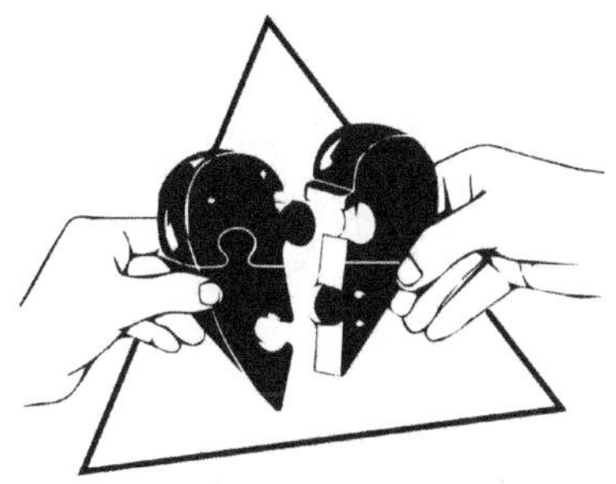

I just sat down after walking miles and miles
And took note of the breeze that blew, the birds
that chirped
And the flowers that bloomed.
But the aphonic ambiance was taken by a storm
And I was left to view the ceasing beauty.
Everything that seemed petty to me then
Got beauty added and were my memoirs of the
last but
Broken silence.
Perhaps all you got to gain and lose are the little
things
That seems petty before they're gone.

The First Stone

The first stone you stepped on when you were
almost to drown
Always holds that place of pride and trust.
Through ages of distance and separation, the
stone today
Bears a rough amount of rust.
Yet, when embellished with the right hands
The stone shines just as the silver lining.
As though some supernatural being made that
stone
When all you could see was a perilous whining
As though some unknown affinity pulled you to
that stone
And you could never make your way out of the
magic.
Possibly living on that stone was the wisest
choice
Yet you moved on to live the next magic.

The second and the third, stone after stone
Ages after ages, as now you returned wrinkled
That stone still floats on the water to welcome
you
With the same shine, it twinkles.
But after years of moving on and passing by
Can you recognize what made you go that far?
If not for the stone that has your footprint on
Your scar would remain just a scar
And mask who you were really meant to be.
If you've failed to thank the stone,
Failed to say how much needed it was
Why don't you thank the support unknown?
And unnoticed and unforgettable?
For your imprint on the stone might be a burden
And it might sink by the time you delay
Deep into where you were to go sunken.

Wish to See The Rainbow

I am a survivor of the storm last night with
umpteen wishes
Final longing for a rainbow
Perhaps all storms have a rainbow that follows,
don't they?
I hid my face under the tree trunk
While my sleeve dripped like my eyes
For I was driven by optimism in the darkest
hour.
I could get back home because the clock struck
twelve
But I wanted to bask myself in the sun
And the wait should be worth it, shouldn't it?

But I didn't really see the rainbow after that
unending pour
I was bestowed with injustice after a night of
survival

I felt betrayed by the cameras that captured
rainbows.

Lo! But turns out I saw the rainbow with my
heart
And it warms me to greet the rainbow of not
mine
But my destiny's fancies. To me, you're one
Who is not the light but the color after the storm.
Perhaps I was awarded much more than what I'd
thought–
I was gifted the gift of humanity–you
More precious than pearls under seas and gold
under soil
To see you in person was a trip back from
eternity.
It began with you and shall continue with you–
the rainbow
I failed to dream of it. For you're not transient
Like the one that appears in the sky. You're the
rainbow
The rich, the poor, the sane, the insane–all seek
for.
You're the rainbow in the day and the star at
night
That guides me home when it strikes twelve.
So, I ain't a survivor of the storm last night,
Let me be the victor for once, at least, rainbow.

For I won what mortals squabble for–the
greatest wealth
The guiding light in my life. And my wish to see
And feel and love and live the rainbow is truer,
each day.

The Path

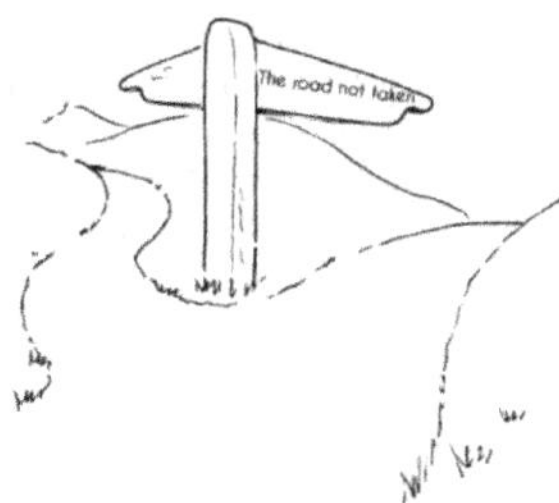

That path, you know which one,
Journeyed only and only once
Twice and thrice and more and more
Have recollections that never suffice.

You look here and you look there,
You look as far as eyes can see
Still the trodden olden path
Has much to give and much to weep.

The one that you had chanced upon,
With the most jocund company
Now all that lies is an olden path
The tread lost amidst our symphony.

If I chance upon that path again
I would ask what more it has
For me to muse and muse all day
Of it and the company, Alas!
Yet to look at the path again
And where I came from and where to go
I pat my back and clap my hand
For the path is much more than I know!

www.ingramcontent.com/pod-product-compliance
Lightning Source LLC
La Vergne TN
LVHW041227200726
843507LV00013B/2603